EXCELLENCE IN ADVISORY TEAMS

EXCELLENCE IN ADVISORY TEAMS

B. VINCENT

CONTENTS

CHAPTER 1

Introduction to Excellence in Advisory Teams

This book approaches the question of how high-performing advisory teams maintain and grow thriving practices. We will explore the unique skills, behaviors, and practices of highly functioning advisory teams and provide a look inside the Supernova method for success. Many professionals thrive in an advisory team, and the fastest growing advisory teams in North America are intentionally considering many of the concepts that will be explored in this book. Investment in an advisory team helps team members move to excellence and define a lifestyle practice, a business practice, or an enterprise practice.

The concept of the Supernova Method, the subject of our book, was introduced in the phrase "Don't be a red giant" by Rob Knapp. This phrase was captured by Mark Goldberg to title an book titled "A Supernova Legacy". So what is Supernova? Supernova is an entity in demise, blow-up of a star, implosion that releases a huge amount of energy, leaving behind a neutron star or a black hole. A supernova is a "wow" experience that captures the audience's attention in a big way. To take that concept into the context of a tornado, which is our workhorse meeting for advisory teams, the term supernova would apply to the initial coaching session and the advisory team's first and big epic event.

Understanding the Importance of Advisory Teams

The best executive is the one who has sense enough to pick good people to do what needs to be done, and self-restraint to keep from meddling when they do it. These words of Theodore Roosevelt bear witness to the enormous importance teams have in the organizational environment. The need to conduct our business in teams is becoming an important fact of life. If we have to expand the organizational periphery, involving employees, suppliers, customers, and lawmakers, we will need the help of advisory teams. Because of this, the effectiveness and efficient functioning in these teams have become crucial. Working in teams contributes directly to overall success and effectiveness by simply bringing more people's talents to bear on a particular project or goal than any one individual could.

An increasingly popular way of resource allocation within large organizations is a project-based approach. One or more experts with specific knowledge of the objectives of the project are amalgamated into an ad-hoc project team that can be put together with other people for other projects on a need-to-know basis. This creates the concept of the Boundaryless Organization. A boundaryless organization achieves excellence in teams. An advisory team is a temporary group made up of specialists from within or without an organization working together on a specific project that has an immediate relevance to a problem of the organization.

Overview of the Supernova Method

The Supernova Method is a roadmap that you and your advisory team can use to build and maintain a business that is a true expression of your calling. This process addresses the four pillars of your business foundation: client experience, money management, investment management, and practice management. You will be able to turn the normally arbitrary thought process of your practice into a quantifiable and clear vision. The Supernova Method allows you to develop an elite team, develop a band of raving followers, and only service the clients you want to. You will be able to develop and deliver a step-by-step game plan process that separates you from the competition.

The Supernova Method is people-focused, meaning that it helps you to understand who you are in relation to your team, your clients, and your business. The Supernova Method is about mindset, the way you think about your business. Your business is not the four walls you go to work in, and it is not a way to pay your bills. Your business is an extension of who you are. It is about bringing your life, family, and business into synergistic harmony. The Supernova Method is both a research methodology to help you understand your business and validate your business components and a planning and implementation process to help you get your business where you want it to be. It is ongoing, not static. It encompasses all the pieces of your business including your team, your clients, and your business operations. It is all-inclusive. It is a method of doing business so that your business nurtures your life, not competes with it. The Supernova Method is flexible in that it can be used with a solo practitioner, a small group of advisors, and with large multi-discipline practice organizations. It is a stand-alone process to be used to build your business and create the life that you want. The Supernova Method CPA will encompass everything in the Supernova Method, but it will place special emphasis on the core competencies of the CPA practitioners. In this manual, we will review topics such as the awakening, the four pillars, the grounding statement, and developing your "Supernova Mind". You will also learn the importance of having a great team and how to use motivational filters to develop your dream team. You will learn how to create effective, "self-wrote" marketing that resonates with you and that clients will find seductive. You will be able to develop your own "WOW" process that makes you extraordinary and helps turn clients into a band of raving attracted followers. To round out your process, you will create and deliver the Wisdom path, a step-by-step investment game plan process that helps develop the buy-in with your center of influence and power visor clients to grow your business exponentially. Instead of trying to be all things to all people, it has helped them to break through their self-imposed limitations to find their niche.

CHAPTER 2

Foundations of Effective Advisory Teams

Foundations of effective advisory teams. To identify the surprising few individuals who can thrive in highly unstructured, non-hierarchical creative teams, ADP members have developed the "field of teams!" Pivotal to the success of the advisory team is the need to balance the cost and manner of recruitment with the revenue generated by and projected delivery of engagements. Great consulting firms place a premium price on the cost/size of their teams to satisfy the delivery of projects.

Expertise in various areas may need to be complemented by expertise in working across domains. Expected to provide consistent and high value-added advice as part of the advisory team, colleagues have to be able to display some common traits and behaviors. While valuing appropriate and collective input to the decision-making process, teams collaborate effectively. Shared responsibility is accepted as they willingly delegate decision-making among themselves. In addition, team members share an explicit and strong commitment to the purpose and direction of the advisory team. They welcome joint review of their strengths and weaknesses and the performance of the team. Inter-group and cross-industry skills underpin the work of advisory teams, and because of this, we need to pay attention to four distinct but interdependent areas of functioning if we are to create a rewarding team experience.

Key Characteristics of High-Performing Teams

The Supernova Companies have discovered that high-performing advisory teams possess a number of unique characteristics essential for excellence. These star teams are proficient in leadership, forthrightness, and accountability, plus a strong belief in human progress. All members should be able to trust one another; as simple as that. They should not have illogical fears like the apprehension of judgment. They trust that if a thought does not tally with theirs, they have to chuck it around and turn it upside down, to shake an idea loose of the irresistible harmonies that seize their thoughts. 'Yes, I believe in humans' can-do-it-and-it-will-not-rain-in-July optimism' implies no Pollyanna principle. The professional advisor who believes in this idea has the officer who stands just before the flight about to take off and believes it is conceivable that it might not crash. Moreover, he signs on. All members of the star advisory team are stubborn. They are relentless when visualizing a target they plan to pursue no matter what. They face adversity with determination and they pass that upon the man.

They welcome conflict. They believe in the efficacy of competition. They joust with each other. They crack each other on the larding of such-and-such an idea, and they like it. They relish a good argument. They enjoy swimming against the tide. In fact, they do not know what to make of someone who does not. They are slaves to some higher goal of exceeding their expectations rather than following. They know how to grow. Everyone knows that growth is vital. People need growth as surely as they need bread and milk. But growth isn't easy. There's a bazillion ways to design an organization for growth. There are unlimited ways to motivate people for growth. But when you cut all the talk apart, the only way people grow is when they are responsible...when they are personally responsible for their growth. So growth, when you get right down to it, is all about responsibility. Super teams must then give everyone the freedom to rise and fall on their own responsibility.

Building Trust and Communication

When working with families, clients, and high net-worth individuals, trust can take years to earn and mere seconds to lose. Each and every member of a family has experienced advisors who have let them down in some way, even if it was just to forget their favorite beverage while in the office or mix up which spouse prefers sugar in their coffee. Consistency can help build a rapport with clients and their spouses, but to work as a team, members need to trust one another even more. Trust ties everything together. It is the bedrock upon which advisory teams are built. It must be there at the core of every employee's soul.

One failure, one hidden truth and the entire flow breaks down. Contact closures do not occur, and professional black holes appear. If an advisory firm has developed a culture of trust between team members, the sky's the limit. If not, all the organizational tools and job descriptions will stop even the best of aspirations. There are no shortcuts for building trust. Is it any wonder that the Supernova team has gone through the painful process of genetically induced personality profiling, multiple day-long retreats with different types of testing and many, many, many "get real" sessions of bringing hidden leadership traits to the surface? Maintaining and developing those open lines of communication are critical to being a valuable and indispensable resource to the families involved. Open lines of communication help teams prioritize efforts and ensure that "all guns are pointed in the same direction" for the planning needs of the families. "Communication" is to "great team" as "oxygen" is to "human being." Need we say more?

CHAPTER 3

The Supernova Method in Practice

The Supernova Method is a proprietary process developed specifically to bring excellence to the advisory teams delivering comprehensive financial advice, and it is the model for an advisory team that is built to scale. Let us consider the contrast between the Low Skill Zone, the Basic Service Zone, and the Ongoing Service Zone and then shift our focus to the difference between the Ongoing Service Zone and the Excellence Zone. Moving from the Low Skill Zone to the Ongoing Service Zone is mostly a matter of perspective and structure. It is possible and practical to do all of the work now that will be done eventually to move an entire operation from the Low Skill Zone and the Basic Service Zone into the Ongoing Service Zone. The Ongoing Relationship System platforms are very likely to break through any performance obstacles that have hindered operations in the past.

Teams that have successfully transitioned from the Ongoing Service Zone to the Excellence Zone are exceptional in the delivery of comprehensive financial, tax, and law advisory services. Teams in the Excellence Zone are also committed to efficiency and profitability, delivering high-value professional services in a scalable way. Let us give some examples of what this looks like in terms of the Customer Journey. A comprehensive financial and tax advice process will cover: goal work, personal financial health check, risk profiling and risk tolerance testing, investment process, pre-retirement strategies, investment advice, life and permanent disability insurance advice, retirement planning, aged care advice, estate planning, personal insurance advice including life insurance and income protection, tax plan and finance advice, and legal advice for wills, enduring guardianships and powers of attorney.

Defining the Supernova Methodology

Supernova Wirehouses and Super RIAs have always enjoyed some advantages over other advisory teams. They often have a larger client base and thus more revenues and profits. As a result of our work with over 150 advisor organizations that utilize a team approach—wirehouses, super RIAs, independent fiduciaries & planning professionals, insurance-affiliates, hybrids, etc., we have learned that when an advisory team is composed of individuals rather than entities, these other advisory teams tend to adhere to what we call the Supernova Method.

Supernova firms are defined by a basic structure that tends to be repeated successfully over and over again. We call this structure the Supernova Method. Just as the periodic table of elements componentizes carbon as carbon only, hydrogen as hydrogen only, plutonium as plutonium only, we have figured out the most basic components of Supernova Teams. Our research has shown that teams following the Supernova Method have been successful in sharing the same team skills, client engagement approach, branding approach, and owner's economic rewards model across teams, businesses, & partnerships. Of course, every team will want or need to customize the program to suit their own particular brand extractions, internal talent, and unique fit in their particular market, but that is the flexibility of what has proven to be a global practice of sound operating principles. Our loose intuition for naming these atomic team components the "Supernova Method" is that just as components of the atom are essentially common amongst all of us, our goal is that Supernova clients see into the "nucleus of team" and that core commonality helps everyone in the world leverage the Supernova brand experience.

Implementation Strategies and Best Practices

The following have been successful in implementing the Supernova Method in an organization:

1. Identify early-pilot teams carefully.

a. Top advisors and teams who "get it".

2. Launch implementation with a "kickoff" event.

a. Cast a vision for the trusted advisor-business model.

b. Create a compelling case for change.

c. Detail the features of the program.

d. Provide a comprehensive "way ahead" plan and timeline.

3. Move new top talent into the Supernova team.

a. Let old teams wither.

b. Gently push early pilots to full implementation.

c. Carefully discuss options with other teams.

Continued Change Management

1. Supernova is only a phase in a longer-term process.

2. For the full firm to support it, continue to talk to everyone.

3. Recognize the experience and contributions of your long-term employees who face such significant modification of their trusted advisor methods.

4. Interact carefully with non-high-end potential tailoring of Supernova.

5. Begin to create Supernova practice-group leads/trusted advisors from within each of these groups/specialties.

6. Implement early steps of the Supernova Method (trusted advisor penetration) with these first-tier clients.

7. Also implement the enhanced design format with first tier clients.

8. Marketing will have to support this thrust, by, among other issues, developing a more sharply focused "dream client profile" for each.

CHAPTER 4

Measuring Success and Continuous Improvement

The vision and strategies for a client-centric engagement are driving the business operations of Supernova Companies Inc. Members of the CEO Roundtable take it as given that the practice of business is to be for the sake of service to and for other people, and that a client-centric engagement involves the continual development of an exemplary relationship with your customer, while evolving expertise, wisdom, and knowledge of how to better help your customer.

The businesses of our members have developed client-centric advisory teams, guided by the 3x5 plan. They are continually developing operational and performance excellence. It was pointed out that this has caused a general shift from the focus on the product, including how products can be improved and added value for customers, to a focus on the complete array of services being offered to the client. This raises the question, "How do you design a client-centric lead generation program when you're focusing on a service that's part of a total package?" Members suggested rephrasing the question to: "What is the lead generation state of the art for world-class advisory teams operating in a truly client-centric environment?" It's essential that the group agrees that the proper definition of a lead in a client-centric environment is any individual who is qualified to commit and has committed to the second meeting in the client-centric sales process. Once the brick was set, the financial institution sought to expose and remove the weak keystone. The roundtable actively sought ways to remain the supreme industry leader – to avoid becoming the weak link that exposes the weak link in the client-centric process. That began the process for Session Two. CEO Roundtable members shared how they assess their teams' success and plan for continuous improvement. Consider these key benchmarks to measure your team's success, and opportunities for ongoing enhancement and evolution.

Key Performance Indicators for Advisory Teams

An organization focuses on its advisory teams in order to offer strategic value to advisors. With a strategy of paying attention and measuring key indicators, your organization becomes capable of identifying what value is being delivered, as well as if changes should be made to those metrics. Offered below are indicators important to measuring the success of advisory teams, along with brief descriptions. A more accurate explanation and evaluation of each measurement can be found in the following portions of the thesis.

Internal staff measurements demonstrate whether the advisory staff are completing tasks efficiently, within budgeted hours. They describe the dynamics of the team and provide an indication of the health and morale of personnel involved.

Management measurements evaluate the effectiveness of the advisory team in managing and overseeing the customer relationship. They offer a measure of process management effectiveness as it relates to the customer.

Finally, customer measurements are the most critical measures describing the true impact and value-added by the advisory organization. They may be difficult to measure, but provide a greater value of service benefit to the customer. In reality, the focus will be on limiting these because of the difficulty of acquiring that value.

Feedback Mechanisms and Adjustments

Once the team-advisor relationship has been set in motion or is already established, it is up to the advisory team to create feedback processes that help measure the effectiveness and efficiency of the advisory team in terms of meeting the near-future needs and overall goals of the advisee. These feedback processes can take the form of surveys, regularly scheduled meetings, informal settings, or web-based feedback systems. Closure processes are also necessary to solidify the "handoffs" of clients amongst the advisory members. With regard to cases where formal feedback sessions are held, advisory members enter the meeting with the client "well informed, i.e., pre-briefed" about the issues that will be discussed in the meeting. Feedback sessions of this caliber can allow for a more open and receptive dialogue that the advisee will be more prone to express his/her feelings and thoughts regarding the performance of the advisory team. In keeping with the pre-briefed theme, other feedback forms or methods should also be shared amongst the team members to ensure that the advises do not receive mixed messages from the advisory team. This would be detrimental to the team-advisor relationship that relies on trust and commitment.

Once feedback has been gathered and assessed, adjustments must be made in an appropriate and timely manner. Different feedback indicators will demonstrate to the advisory team what areas of performance and team-interactions the reasons for grievances stem from. After the advisee feedback is processed and presented properly, adjustments can be made according to the reason for the advisee's dissatisfaction. If a lawsuit or complaint might follow the advisee's advice, the process should not be delayed, as complaints left unattended can damage the advisor's rapport with current and prospective clients.

CHAPTER 5

Case Studies and Real-World Applications

Evolution of the supernova method: A case in point

Applied to modern advisory teams, the supernova model must also consider the characteristics of 21st century advice. In summary, clients expect to be provided with "trusted advice" and an "unbiased analysis", but this advice is no longer just financial advice. Instead, it is truly holistic in nature - to meet the quadruple bottom line. Our research has found limited evidence of the supernova concept applied outside of practice management, and certainly not as a framework that describes genuinely "best practice" in an advisory business or team. Our plan is to apply the supernova concept to the analysis of high-performing advisory teams within Australia.

Case study examples

Below are two samples of case studies co-authored by members of the Supernova Research Team, and published by the Financial Planning Association of Australia.

Titan vs Supernova: A comparison of two top financial planning practices

This case study, featuring principal author Justin Jehne, is the story of two very distinct planning practices building successful businesses in the Sydney financial services market.

Crescent Wealth: You don't have to be a big fish to make a splash

This keepsake is the story of (at the time) a two-year-old start-up that is changing the way some of the nation's 1.3 million Muslims think about and approach their finances. The "by Muslims, for Muslims" organisation provides superannuation and zero-interest property funding to Australia's growing Muslim community.

Success Stories from Organizations Implementing the Supernova Method

Numerous case studies and stories were presented about the methods and processes discussed in this article. While the stories shared in this paper are encouraging, formal research to validate the results is ongoing. We found no evidence that any of those sharing the stories are expert consultants, and we do not recommend or endorse the quality of advisement they provide. We share these anecdotal success stories to encourage advisors that success is happening around them. "The Supernova Method, as laid out in the book, is awesome. It is helping me to get to the next level in my business. Making change is painful... especially at first. But the benefits far outweigh the pain in this instance. Thanks for putting it out."

The combination of the Supernova Model and the Supernova Method is helping financial advisory teams at all levels across the country. New advisors who embrace the model quickly arrive at capacity levels of $40-$60 million per relationship because they become Supernova Advisors. A planned practice attracts planned clients. This allows advisors to hire to their model of planning and managing wealth, not moonlighting as a social worker. Seasoned financial professionals at established and fledgling teams are able to become more efficient and pull money off of their servicing desks to enter into a charge-based planning model. The increase in planning fees more than outweighs the decrease in their 12c-1 fees. Less time combined with more dollars equals considerable profitability. A Kansas City broker-dealer recently increased fees by 50% and simultaneously went up in assets to clients! In four months, they put on over $200 million in client assets.

CHAPTER 6

Challenges and Solutions in Advisory Teams

This article primarily deals with combining different production factors in one group to increase the competitiveness of the financial services market. Although the initial study provides in-depth empirical evidence about a company managed by individual professionals, other areas of advisory services are sometimes encountered. The study provided evidence that most cases of advice were given in groups, consisting of a group, even where each manager also managed the private risk on sensitive matters. Establishing a partnership on the basis of different qualifications creates conflict within the team for identifying the base group and team settings.

Despite the increase in the market, I found that the members of a group jointly produce what actually creates specialization and is independent of both the qualifications of individual advisors and the special features of the individual manager. Thus, over time, the conditions for developing a new way of grouping firms that cannot be a brand or an easily identified sector are seen within a coastal area can be created, and it is advisable to also create collective specialization within the sector to ensure that beneficiary stakeholders rely on embarking on their investment funds in a slowly growing economy.

The range and scope of financial advisory services that can be performed by a company depends on the depth and general scope of the knowledge and the sharing position we have within the team, rather than on a separate group. Moreover, thanks to the joint participation in the management and the activities of the team, each single manager has a dual status for those who are on a money protection foundation. This "shared assumption" creates resilience and adaptability, which enable individuals and teams to adapt to changes and find more creative solutions to problems.

Common Pitfalls and How to Avoid Them

It has become clear that there are several common pitfalls in leading an advisory team, including lack of ease in the operational, delegation to others, too much centralization, and managing by consensus are all frequent problems. Here are some helpful hints that will aid in preventing these pitfalls and overcoming them if they arise.

Being stuck in the minutia and too central to most half-hearted efforts. Delegate work to other people. Typically, as coordinator of the advisory staff, you are the primary point of call for others in the workforce. Since you are off mat, everything must come to a standstill if you are away. You may be delegated responsibility for a job just as any other member of the advisory team. You're not required to do so on your own. Delegate the administration and the forms to the appropriate person. Additionally, rather than always having to render decisions for others, instruct them to start guiding their clients so that they may pick up the slack and find guidance from you. If in doubt of something, you can still be notified in order to ensure that all is in line with your approach and to reject any efforts to reinvent the wheel.

Reject managing by committee. Each individual member of the team does not have to like or share your decisions when the going gets tough. In fact, any squad should have a range of viewpoints that should be endorsed. Typically a common outcome would not be easy to achieve. Just make a decision and press forward. If required, you may automatically handle any fallout.

Deliberate Abuse. During their infancy, many consultancies are managed by their indispensable leader in a serial harassing manner. Everything must be reviewed by the "guy at the best" a variation of the "damn details" pitfall. A more intrusive as well as costly version of this approach is dictating outcome, which includes dictating terms to the rest of the team on a number of things to be accomplished based the way you would. clerical people to secretary. Hire administrative staff, such as secretarial or goal bookkeeper onboarding persons, filing clerks, etc. All are necessary In Seek to reduce this dependence on capturing, scanning, etc. Other specialists to office assistants. Presently the official assistant of the CFO is the human means manager, who has a part-time control function with no professional job-relevant training. Executives were frequently slow in receiving help until they were struggling to cope, whereas our clients are now working on developing the hiring of the next generation leading their infrastructure and operational stuff as a top priority and reluctance and not to walk carelessly, confidently and non-produdgressively, towards them, and confidently and unia-limm.

Resilience and Adaptability in Team Dynamics

A secondary set of qualities often determines the quality of the navigation approach when working with advisory teams. These qualities, which could be referred to as being adaptive or resilient, are of great importance to members, as they allow them to work around the system and still accomplish their goals. Exploring these kinds of strategies, of course, can be complex and are not without difficulty, yet attributes relating to adaptability and resilience seem to be instrumental to comprehending team - or network - dynamics.

One possible approach to doing so comes from common themes that seem to arise from the diverse set of activities represented in the narratives provided by team members participating in our interviews. Themes that we might invest time in developing seem to point to a reduction in our attraction to universality as a new framework would be grounded in the values of co-production, openness, and respect for multiple realities. Post publication, this research will be used as the bedrock for the development of a video animation aimed at high school students. Team members often start their time on teams with plans for precise goals, focusing on very specific, individual activities. However, they are capable of adjusting to changing conditions and stakeholder demands in ways that are pertinent to their individual situation, not necessarily tied to the direction of a project.

CHAPTER 7

The Future of Advisory Teams and the Supernova Met

If you could see into the future, which trends do you believe would shape the future of advisory teams in the next 10 years? What new tools and insights do you think might arise that could be worked into a Supernova Method to prepare those in the financial planning profession for continued success?

The future of advisory teams will continue to evolve based on the next generation of team members and clients. The desire for digital interaction and automation is already driving significant change across our industry. As advisory teams seek to continuously improve, a more stringent focus on available and future financial planning and advisory services that solve client needs rather than just meeting goals will continue to evolve. Also, co-creating services and products that are built to address areas that current clients don't even know will be a need will also make its appearance as financial planners work to provide solutions.

As an influx of baby boomers fully experience retirement, paying great attention to potential changes in our healthcare system, the financial planner that solves problems related to longevity while being heavily involved and advocating for potential life-extending tools and services will also continue to consolidate around a financial planning focus where financial well-being is a solution and not merely an end-result. The Supernova Advisory Teams advantage will lie in an even greater focus on a full care model of financial planning. A strategic role of a financial planner is the ability to facilitate a client's setting and understanding of their complete life goals and then financially mapping not just solutions but multiple options to how a client can best use their resources within their lifetimes. This will involve helping them understand their current money mindsets and then expanding into putting tools, processes, and habits into place that free clients up to continue capturing joyful, experiential moments. Improving existing tools and refining communication around the processes involved in a Life-planned approach in a world filled with client sleep disorders, anxiety, and fatigue will also be a part of our digital offerings and live events in the Supernova Method.

Trends and Innovations in Team Collaboration

Much is unknown in the financial services industry. While you might have a strong sense of the challenges and inefficiencies that obstruct your path forward, the regular publication of Trends and Innovations can put data-driven analysis behind your decisions. This weekly series explores the latest developments in collaborative work, team efficiencies, and productivity. It looks at new organizational structures and ways of working together. It considers the particular challenges of advisory teams, like the underlying need to manage intangible dynamics. Trends and Innovations also introduces the Supernova Method regularly as an applied perspective on team collaboration for financial consultants, advisors, wealth managers, or anyone working on team-based, intangibles-rich projects.

Read back through Trends and Innovations for the last few months to catch up on the assessment of your capabilities, both collectively and individually, to embrace the future of work. If the trends I've tracked appeal to you, or if they scare you, consider looking into the Supernova Clusters launching globally and see if that intentional learning network might be a good fit for getting you ready to thrive in a workplace and workforce that reward collaboration.

CHAPTER 8

Conclusion and Key Takeaways

Throughout this book, we have discussed in detail the potential that can arise when advisory teams are capable of achieving excellence. We start by defining an advisory team and discussing what it takes to generate unnecessary results. After carefully articulating the implications of decent versus excellent teams, we explained each component of the Supernova model at length. This is the essential structure underlying all advisory team excellence. The five-step method of identifying the client base, segmenting that base into four atomic customer groups, and solidifying trustees and asset allocation rules has been proven across just about every peer system in our industry to be the critical success factor in a team's ability to move to the next level. It describes the secret sauce that an otherwise well-governed and sophisticated RIA operation must have to become truly exceptional.

Too many times we discuss the profitability game on a production basis instead of focusing on the true bottom line impact. After going through the exercise of quantifying the concepts presented in this book, the true power of the premise begins to manifest itself. It's one thing to understand the theory – but what are you going to do about it? The Supernova program has evolved into the most practical "next steps" approach in the industry. While the Supernova program historically has focused on developing new business structures as well as growing and enhancing client relationships, the program has many implications for building an organization's support structure. The goal – to exceed the client's service expectations. We know for a fact – through surveys, focus groups, and other client feedback loops – that our service delivery systems accurately predict excellent financial performance in the client-aggregates that choose to invest with us. The value of the approach is easily quantified by each individual advisor or broker in terms of the current size of the book vs. the size of the book if a high-level client program were implemented.